Reset Your Mindset

15 Success Secrets that Go Beyond Positive Thinking & The Law of Attraction

ADRIENNE N. HEW

Copyright © 2012 Ho'olana Press

All rights reserved.

ISBN: 147755968X
ISBN-13: 978-1477559680

DEDICATION

To all the people who said I couldn't do it

DISCLAIMER

The information contained in **Reset Your Mindset** is intended to serve as a collection of time-tested and proven success strategies.

Summaries, strategies, tips and tricks are only recommendations by the author, and reading this book does not guarantee that one's results will exactly mirror her own results. The author of **Reset Your Mindset** has made all reasonable efforts to provide current and accurate information for the readers of this book. The author will not be held liable for any unintentional errors or omissions that may be found.

The material in **Reset Your Mindset** may include information, products, or services by third parties. Third Party materials comprise of the products and opinions expressed by their owners. As such, the author of this guide does not assume responsibility or liability for any Third Party Material or opinions.

The publication of such Third Party materials does not constitute the authors guarantee of any information, instruction, opinion, products or service contained within the Third Party Material. Use of recommended Third Party Material does not guarantee that your results with **Reset Your Mindset** will mirror that of the author. Publication of such Third Party Material is simply a recommendation and expression of the author's own opinion of that material.

Whether because of the general evolution of the Internet or the unforeseen changes in company policy and editorial submission guidelines, what is stated as fact at the time of this writing, may become outdated or simply inapplicable at a later date. This may apply to **Reset Your Mindset** as well as the various similar companies that have been referenced in this book. Great effort has been exerted to safeguard the accuracy of this writing.

No part of this publication shall be reproduced, transmitted or resold in whole or in part in any form, without the prior written consent of the author. All trademarks and registered trademarks appearing in **Reset Your Mindset** are the property of their respective owners.

ACKNOWLEDGMENTS

I would like to personally thank, Kris Ferraro, who has helped me to further my understanding of both myself and human behavior in general. Your commitment to self-improvement and creating the reality you want is truly an inspiration.

I am also grateful to my husband, Joseph Brown, for editing this book while helping me to stay true to my voice.

Table of Contents

1 - The Road to Freedom 1

2 - My Story 5

3 - You Are Lucky 11

4 - Reasons vs. Excuses: Why Some People Find Success So Hard 13

5 - The College Professor 17

6 - The Judge 23

7 - The Separatist and The Joiner 31

8 - The Confidant(e) 37

9 - The Pauper 41

10 - The Tycoon-In-Training 49

11 - The Cynic 53

12 - The Multi-Tasker 59

13 - The Old Fuddy-Duddy 65

14 - The Workaholic 69

15 - The Naysayer 73

16 - A Good Use of Ego 77

17 - Lesson from Babes: Finding a Place for Failure 81

18 - The Challenge 83

Final Notes and Resources 85

ABOUT THE AUTHOR 87

1 - The Road to Freedom

"The whole secret of existence is to have no fear. Never fear what will become of you, depend on no one. Only the moment you reject all help are you freed."
- Buddha

There are many teachings available today aimed at helping people achieve financial success through unconventional methods. Whether reading "law of attraction" books or books about making gobs of money overnight, people are eager to live the dream of making more money while having more time to spend with family and friends or traveling the world.

However, when most people attempt to implement the concepts from such books or movies, they often fall far short of their intentions and quickly dismiss these teachings as a sham or sensationalized nonsense that is meant to take advantage of gullible dreamers. Nothing could be further from the truth!

What they do not realize is that most people suffer from negative self-talk. They continually send themselves subtle messages of failure and hardship that can easily undo any good intentions they have for their success.

Like most people, my life has had some awesome successes and some pathetic failures. Looking back, it is easy to identify those thoughts and behaviors that launched me to the next level of prosperity and those that kept me stagnant

In recent years, I have learned to focus more on the types of actions and thinking that more consistently produce positive results. The truth is it only takes subtle changes in mindset and perspective to be successful.

In this book, I will share with you how the way I think today has helped me achieve these successes and how you can turn things around for yourself, if you feel stuck.

This is not a book about strategies for making money. It is about the way you think about money and explores the many reasons why money may not flow to you very easily. At the end of the book, I will provide the name of one of my favorite books for generating money-making ideas.

Now while this book focuses on financial wealth, the principles can absolutely be applied to other areas of your life such as health and your overall wellbeing and happiness. As you read through each section, you may become aware of places in your life where you unconsciously decide to adopt a vow of poverty in terms of your emotions, health or spirituality for example. Luckily you can apply the same solutions for resolving your money issues to these other areas of your life as well.

There are many roads that can lead to success, if you apply the right mindset. I chose Internet marketing as my way of automating income, so there will be many references to this industry throughout the coming pages. In case you need an explanation, Internet marketing is the process of generating money online through websites such as e-commerce stores, review sites that get referral commissions, membership sites, selling ad space or any number of other sales models. I find it fun and exciting to crack the code of making money with this method.

It is up to you to decide which money-making method rings true for you. What are those phrases you found yourself uttering to friends over and over again? "I wish I didn't have a boss.", "I wish somebody would invent....", "I would love to..." If you have found yourself a victim of the current recession or lay offs at your job, you especially need to tune into these thoughts. The Universe is simply responding to your deepest desires by discontinuing the stagnant relationship that was your job. So now, what are you going to do with this opportunity? Trade it in for another job? Or step up to the challenge and make your dreams come true?

2 - My Story

*"If you've heard this story before,
don't stop me because I'd like to hear it again."*
- Groucho Marx

Not everyone finds the road to success easy. I did not in the beginning.

Like most people, I come from a long line of hard workers. People in my family define themselves by the amount of work they do, what job titles they have and how much money they bring home. As someone who has always found learning even the most obscure concepts relatively easy, family members had a lot of hope riding on me from an early age.

However, after graduating from New York University with a Bachelor of Arts in French and Spanish, I floundered for years in a series of conventional jobs.

Over the years, I had tried my hand at everything from trade show coordinator to professional belly dancer, but despite my sincere interest in these areas, nothing felt right.

Nothing felt like "the thing" I would want to do for the rest of my life. I was always just passing time until the next hobby-turned-career presented itself.

Along the way, I had suffered a serious health crisis. A sort of blessing in disguise that woke me up to the virtues of real nutrition. It was a far cry from the politically correct way that the government and some special interest organizations would have us eat, but a way of nourishing the body that actually heals the body. Had it not been for this crisis -- or at least my persistence to heal it -- I would not be here today.

At the urging of my doctor who taught me how to eat to feed my body properly, I went back to school for holistic nutrition. This made sense to me because from a very young age, I had an interest in real cooking that did not involve a lot of processed, pre-packaged items.[1] Exactly what my body had apparently been craving all along.

After earning my degree as a Certified Nutritionist, I figured that perhaps now I would find my calling in this seemingly lucrative and in-demand field. But when I opened my practice, I found one fatal flaw -- I hated working with clients! I quickly found out that most people were not interested in health, they wanted quick, easy solutions to what they thought was their health problem, not what their lab tests showed and certainly not what my professional expertise noted. They did not want to take supplements. They did not want to eat real food no matter how delicious they told me it was. They wanted drugs.

So there I was with a brand new, specialized degree in a field that I had a true calling for, but unable to turn it into a

---

[1] Actually, I wanted to know how the heck Maryanne on Gilligan's Island could make all those coconut cream pies without the aid of supermarket ingredients. Seriously, how did she do it?

sustainable living without compromising my values or driving myself insane.

Back to the drawing board.

Just as I considered throwing in the towel, I started thinking of moving my business online and finally getting on track.

Getting set up online was not the easiest road to success though. The first course I took in Internet marketing was indirectly recommended by a friend and sadly turned out to be a complete scam.

Setting up my business using the model I was taught felt false and disingenuous. And my results were abysmal, probably because I felt sleazy promoting myself using these tactics.

It would have been all too easy to just give up at this point, but there was something about Internet marketing that drove me to pursue it further. Internet marketing offered me what I had always wanted, but was too afraid to ask for -- a scalable way to make money without a boss and without the guesswork of trying to figure out what clients wanted. Had I been in the wrong mindset, I would have never recognized the potential for this relatively easy business model.

Fearing that I had damaged my reputation as a nutritionist, I walked away from my nutrition practice in order to decode the many theories and strategies needed for marketing a small business on the Internet. It took some time, but two years later, I am finally profitable in my Internet and nutrition businesses.

Looking back at the series of events that led up to my current success, I can now identify those behaviors that have consistently produced positive results and those unconscious actions that have caused me great misery and disappointment.

This book, however, is not about me. It is about you. It is about us. It is about human behavior. It is about the ego and how it controls our ability to fail or succeed.

The ego is that part of our subconscious that seeks drama. The ego is responsible for the emotions we express. Many of these emotions keep us in a state of stagnation and procrastination. The ego likes to complain, get angry, create controversy, place blame, call names, be right at all costs and otherwise invent problems. It is the story we tell about ourselves. Yes, much like the story I am telling you right now.

However, the ego can also mask itself as happiness. Many times, the ego uses false happiness to ignore reality. This may seem confusing, but it is not when you consider how easily seemingly positive emotions such as happiness and love can turn into negative ones such as sadness, anger or hate. The opposite of all these emotions is indifference, what some might call "zen".

One mom I know, for example, is always so happy and smiling whenever she talks about her kids. She believes they are beautiful and that everybody agrees with this assessment. Her kids, however, are well known bullies with other children. Unfortunately she cannot recognize this dysfunction because she does not understand that her happiness is not the opposite of what most parents would probably express as anger. Telling herself the story of how wonderful her children are is just as dysfunctional as another parent that might tell herself how horrible the same child is.

In case you were wondering, yes, the ego is quite schizophrenic in nature. It possesses many personalities that surface when your conscious self is not paying attention. This book will introduce you to several of your inner personalities. Personalities you may not even be aware exist. The aim is not to point fingers at you and make you feel bad about yourself or hopeless to ever gain dominion over them. Instead, recognizing their possible existence will help bring awareness to your actions, which is the first step in making progress.

So-called positive and negative emotions give the ego a purpose, which ensures its survival. Without the continuous influx of extreme emotions, the ego dies and we remain realistic instead of reactive to our circumstances. When we are realistic, it is easy to find solutions to life's challenges because we are not caught up in a story that judges the event. We are indifferent.

Indifference is a state of being free of the ego.

By analyzing how the ego plays a role in your success or failure in life, you will get an in-depth look at how we as humans think and why we think what we think. It is an analysis of those fleeting thoughts and subconscious ideas that prevent us from fully realizing our potential. It is why we face the hurdles we do in areas of our lives where success is measured in terms of money, choice, time and/or overall happiness.

Our egos can cause us to spin our wheels, procrastinate and sabotage our efforts to attain our goals. Only by confronting and understanding our ego are we able to jump over those hurdles to achieve the previously unthinkable. This is the state of consciousness. Bringing consciousness to those times when the ego is taking over is the only way to eventually become free of it.

For some people, this will all read like metaphysical hogwash. For others, they will find objection after objection why they are the one exception to all the examples and ideas laid out in the coming pages. But hopefully, the ideas in these pages will resonate with the majority of you and give you the tools you need to end destructive behaviors that impact your financial future.

I assure you that if any of what you read here makes you feel uncomfortable, it is for one reason...it is true. We typically only get angry and uncomfortable with what we fear might be true. Just as it is uncomfortable for most people to look themselves in the mirror with a straight face and say "I love you" out loud, any discomfort you experience when taking this honest look at yourself is simply resistance of the ego faced with the reality that it may not be able to run the "woe-is-me" show for much longer. Instead it must take a back seat to the higher you that recognizes success as the only option going forward.

With that, let's get started. I have a lot to say.

3 - You Are Lucky

"If one is lucky, a solitary fantasy can totally transform one million realities."
-Maya Angelou

Before we get into the real nitty-gritty, I would like to point out to you just how lucky you are. Yes, you! If you are reading this you are lucky... very lucky. Not because you have the privilege of reading the words I am writing, but because you have been born into an age of rapid communication and luxury unparalleled at any time in history.

In no other time in mankind's existence has it been as simple as it is today for the common person, regardless of age, ethnicity, race or religion, to chart his or her own course in life. The Internet, in particular, has put the sharing of ideas and many revolutionary monetization methods literally at our fingertips.

If you live in the United States, you are particularly lucky because you live in a society founded upon the ideas of dreamers from long ago. Despite its youthful age, the United

States quickly became one of the wealthiest countries on the planet because of the ingenuity of its people and the encouragement of its citizens to innovate and bring to fruition concepts that were previously thought unimaginable.

The United States was not only the first of the British colonies to win independence from Great Britain, but it has been the birthplace of innumerable inventions that seemed impossible and even crazy before they came to fruition. From the electric light bulb and moving pictures to the airplane and the Internet, the U.S. has been firmly established as a place where anything is possible.

There is a strange dichotomy, however, to living in the United States. On the one hand, you are expected to dream to be anything you want to be. On the other hand, you are expected to work your fingers to the bone, find a reliable job and settle down in the neighborhood where you grew up.

I would like to challenge the latter by telling you that it is your duty as an American to dream and to dream big. Do not allow your wildest dreams to be squashed because you fear coming across as unrealistic or simply nuts. And do not let your forebears down by allowing yourself to be stifled by modern expectations of "knowing your place" or being so practical that you never take the leap of faith to dream outside the box.

If you live in any other country in the world, you are also quite lucky. The fact that you have access to electricity and rapid communication methods proves that. Although your fellow countrymen might be a bit more conservative in their expectations of what is possible in this life, you are lucky because you dare to break free of the constraints of conventional society and venture into the unknown.

Once you realize just how lucky you are, you will recognize that nothing can hold you back. The cards are stacked in your favor. You only need accept it and go with the flow. Everything will fall into place.

4 - Reasons vs. Excuses: Why Some People Find Success So Hard

"An excuse is worse and more terrible than a lie, for an excuse is a lie guarded." - Pope John Paul II

There are many reasons why people cannot seem to get ahead in life. And most of them, some might say all of them, stem from the ego's attempt to create drama in your life where there is none. The ego dies if drama does not exist and survival is the ego's number one goal.

Interestingly enough, whatever we identify as our reasons for failure to achieve greater things are frequently not reasons, but excuses.

Reasons are valid circumstances, which are probably beyond your control or you are not aware of, that may stand in your way of getting something done in a timely fashion. Something such as a flood in your workspace, a power outage, or a death in the family are true reasons why you cannot get your work done (although depending on how long they go on they can turn into excuses). In short, reasons are facts when viewed honestly -- no drama or special interest attached.

Excuses, on the other hand, are more like alibis we identify as the reason for falling short of our goals, but are usually within our control. The phone kept ringing off the hook, I cannot find any help, my watch stopped working etc. These are typical excuses. Unless you absolutely need to answer the phone, then turn the phone off or keep your conversations short. If you cannot find help, you will either need to stop to take time to find help or just go a bit slower -- don't give up entirely. And if your watch is not working, then look up the time on your computer or another clock around the house. Clocks are on everything these days.

Therefore every time you think you have identified a reason why you cannot meet your goals, take a few moments to acknowledge whether it is a reason or an excuse. The real reasons for not getting ahead are those of which you are most likely unaware, so you may need to delve a bit deeper than the surface.

We all have excuses that we use and I frequently have to catch myself in the act of looking for reasons not to complete projects. For most of us, it is an ongoing process to get ourselves aware of our own behavior.

I am often astounded at how unaware people are of their actions. Since the U.S. economy started tanking over a decade ago, I have known more than just a few people who have either lost their homes or been on the verge of foreclosure or bankruptcy. And in each case, it was completely avoidable.

If someone cannot afford to pay their mortgage, do they really need to spend $500 on a weekend in a fancy hotel in Chicago ordering room service and renting movies? No.

Does someone actually need a landline phone AND an iPhone if it has nothing to do with providing them a means by which they can pay their bills? No.

Does someone really need a cruise to the Caribbean just because their friends are going despite the fact that a relative has to pay their mortgage for them? No.

One person argued that he only spent $40 on dinner in a restaurant once per week, even though he could not afford the insurance on his car. Eating the same meal at home handily could save him $100 per month.

Another friend recently came to me "in need" because she had been out of work for almost two years. For less than $35, I was able to buy a family of four a week's worth of mostly organic groceries including meat, eggs, butter, vegetables and a few staples.

Of course, once I realized that she was buying fast food like fries and pizza on an almost daily basis, the gravy train ended. For the cost of two containers of French fries (at a cost of about 79 cents each), she could have fed her entire family each a slice of bread and half a dozen of organic eggs (perhaps not top quality organic eggs, but you get the picture).

Each one of these people had complaints about how someone else was the cause of their misery: how their customers did not pay their bills; how they needed to treat themselves to something because of a birthday or holiday; how a competing company was taking their customers; how illegal aliens were taking all the jobs (little do they realize that illegals typically take the most menial jobs that most Americans would never do); and on and on.

But how can we achieve any kind of success when we turn all the power over to others? If a non-paying customer were so powerful, they would not feel compelled to rip someone else off for a job well done. If a competing company were so powerful, they would not need to lie, cheat or spy on your business. If an illegal alien were so powerful, then they would be legal!

Looking at what others are doing is the best way to become a failure. Not the kind of failure that learns from their mistakes, but a true failure to achieve anything more than one's own current situation. These excuses are nothing, but distractions. Do not allow yourself to become distracted by others. By caring so much about what others are doing, you dilute your own ability to think creatively and move forward.

It is all too easy to allow the ego to deceive us into thinking that we have no power over our own destiny. Perhaps worse, it is easy to buy into the concept that the actions or choices of others who have absolutely no relation to our own lives somehow make it impossible for us to get ahead or live in peace.

Know that you already have all the tools you need to become a success -- however you define success. No doubt you have read, seen a movie or at least heard of someone like Helen Keller who overcame seemingly insurmountable odds to achieve the unimaginable despite complete blindness and deafness since birth. Chances are you are not blind or deaf, so what is holding you back from being all that you can be?

You probably already know what excuses you use to not get ahead. So in addition to learning about your ego's aforementioned multiple personalities, here you will also learn about some of the key reasons why you cannot seem to succeed. Once you identify these underlying reasons and hidden multiple personalities, you can figure out how to deal with them and turn things around.

5 - The College Professor

"Great leaders are almost always great simplifiers, who can cut through argument, debate and doubt, to offer a solution everybody can understand."
- Colin Powell

Every year various news outlets report on the number of billionaires who did not graduate from college. Some never even attended one day of college. Those who consistently make the list are Bill Gates of Microsoft, investment wiz Warren Buffet, Richard Branson of Virgin (Records, Airways and 300 other companies) and former presidential candidate Ross Perot.

When questioned about the reasons for their success, the answers are consistent: they took action and they kept things simple. No fancy college degrees in business administration required.

When I began working online, I noticed a trend of really young guys making a go of online businesses while still in college or in lieu of college. What did they have that I did not? Why were they moving ahead at lightening speed while I was not?

Why was I struggling while these young whipper snappers were making all the money? After all, I have a college degree! Actually, I have several degrees and specialized certificates.

One clear reason is because they are gifted with having been born into the early Internet age and "speak computer" more natively than I. Their interactions online are more intuitive than for those of us who were writing letters and term papers by hand or on a typewriter until they reached their late teens.

At the age of 42, I have been quite proficient in computers and even programming since my teens. Yet I got my start comparatively late and so I still have somewhat of a mental block.

Another reason why these young guys were succeeding so easily is that they were selling things their peers would understand and value. They were working in niches like gaming, ringtones and music-related paraphernalia.

On the other hand, I was using complicated systems and selling items such as e-books that my peers did not trust enough to download to their computers. I would not have even patronized many of these things before I knew anything about Internet marketing. So how could I relate to my peers that it was okay to buy this stuff or click on my referral links or products? I was using all of my energy to sound well-informed and write flawless articles, but still, the rewards were few and far between.

These younger marketers did not have all those years invested in the promise of what a college education would mean for their lives. And if they did, the past decade of global economic hardship likely woke them up to the realities of how little their college degrees mattered in today's work world.

All in all, most of these young guys take the information they learn about marketing and apply it immediately. They don't waste time thinking, they just do.

My one-year old daughter is the same way. If I could get as much done in a day as she does in 10 minutes, I would have been wildly rich five years ago. In the time it takes me to brush my teeth, she can open up a few bottles of hair care products, pull down half the toys in her room and move them into another room.

Give her another minute and should could go up and down the stairs a few times and tear apart one of my plants.

What is my point here? Actually there are two:

First, do *not* overcomplicate things. If you have a college degree, great! But do not think that all roads to success are like researching your dissertation (this only matters if you are in a niche like law or health where you position yourself as an authority and could be sued for false information or claims). It Is okay not to show your smarts or go the extra mile every time in every type of business. You do not want to put out a completely amateurish product or service, but you do not have to make it a masterpiece with every detail "just so". If you do, you will never get started.

In my old neighborhood, I had a friend named Linda. Linda would criticize everyone else's home.

She would talk about how such and such was a slob, how this or that was filthy, how other people couldn't get organized. She would always express how for her, her home, car and clothing would need to be "just so".

Now Linda was not the snappiest of dressers. In fact, she often looked like it was laundry day and she was down to her last pair of sweats. Her car was disheveled and dirty, but who was I to talk?

But I was absolutely horrified the first time I went to her house to find that her house was a complete disaster. It was like Oscar Madison of the Odd Couple met Hoarders. It smelled of dog, bird and cat. There was not only dirt all over the floor, but feathers, pet hair, food, ashes, papers, you name it.

Linda's obsession with making things "just so" put her into a state of paralysis to the point that she did not do anything. She once admitted that she did not clean because if it could not be perfect, she did not have the drive to start the job.

Linda may seem extreme and even insane, but the reality is that her behavior resides in all of us in one way or another. So if you want to be successful at anything you set out to accomplish, do not be a Linda. Do not wait for everything to be "just so" or you will never get anything done.

Secondly, be purposeful and fast. As top marketer Maria Gudelis says "Money loves speed." Draw up your game plan and put it into action.

Try not to get sidetracked by insignificant tasks that are not terribly important to your overall goal. Email, Facebook, TV, radio, and telephone are all common distractions we all give in to at one time or another. Turn them off whenever possible or check in with them at specific times of day, if possible, so you can take the fastest action possible.

I used to sit back contemplating exactly how I was going to do something or think about how unpleasant a certain task or hurdle would be to the point that I would psych myself out and the task would always seem so much more unpleasant and time-consuming.

Now, when I have items to complete, I simply note what has to be done and complete them. I do not give them any power over me (as much as possible). I am the boss of my to-do list, not the other way around.

EXERCISE:

1. **Declutter your workspace.** This is a major distraction. Seeing all the things that need attention around you will keep your mind wandering and provide a great excuse to not get things done.

Removing all the junk from your desk will also invite the Universe to provide more for you. Think about it this way, if you currently have a lot, would the Universe want to overwhelm you by giving you even more stuff? No way! Remove the unimportant stuff to put yourself into receiving mode.

2. **Keep a list of tasks and stick to it.** It seems simple, but so many people ignore this. For the longest time I just tried to keep everything in my head or randomly would write them down in various places. Find a notebook. It doesn't matter if it's particularly attractive or not. What does matter is that you designate this book to jotting down your daily to-do list. How you segment it is up to you. I like to put priority tasks for the following day on one side and long-term tasks on the other side of the same page. I actually label the long-term side "Universe", while the short-term side says "Adrienne". I work on my immediate stuff and trust that the Universe will either get the other side done or at least put into motion the foundation to make my job get smoother once I get around to tackling that long-term task.

3. **Update your list every day at the end of the day and make sure to pat yourself on the back.** Before bed, write down everything you want to get done on the following day. Be reasonable with yourself and make sure that you can actually get those things done within the time you are allotted for working that day. Also, make sure to track your progress by checking off those items you achieved that day. This makes you realize just how far you have come and demonstrates that you are indeed making progress toward the greater good.

MORAL:

You are not perfect. No one is. Instead of criticizing other people's sloppy work or unprofessional demeanor and analyzing what you believe others are doing wrong, realize that those people are a lot closer to success than you because they are taking action. Focus on doing what you need to generate money. Then go back and tweak it as time allows. Again, unless you make money as a lawyer, doctor, construction worker or another area where a wrong decision can cost someone their life, Ready-Fire-Aim is probably just fine.

6 - The Judge

*"There is nothing either good or bad,
but thinking makes it so."*
- Shakespeare, *Hamlet*

Humans use nouns and adjectives to label our world -- house, car, rock, ocean, stormy, flowing, sturdy etc. In terms of nouns, they allow us to identify a person, place or thing that we would like to make reference to. Adjectives on the other hand, allow us to describe the quality of those nouns. However, no single word or combination of sounds can summarize what something, someone or somewhere is. Words give us ideas of the world around us, but they cannot truly convey the deeper meaning of what we are observing.

Nonetheless, judging the world, that is to say segregating the world into opposing sides, such as good and bad, right and wrong, true and false, can be a compulsion for human beings. While judgment at times may be a vital tool in decision-making, it can also be the root of much pain and conflict.

Strong identification with labels is counterproductive to all areas of our lives. When we try to label whether our actions are right or wrong, good or bad, we begin to overanalyze and doubt ourselves. This is a dream-killer for people who are seeking a path to financial independence. These are absolute terms that do not leave a lot of room for debate. And so, we procrastinate and spin our wheels instead of taking action towards our goals.

But that is not all. When we enter a state of judgment, we forfeit our creativity. More often than not, judgment causes us to focus on what we do not want -- pain -- instead of focusing on what we do want, which is pleasure. When we focus on trying to avoid pain, we become irrational, falling prone to making decisions that are unlikely to increase pleasure. Becoming successful at anything depends on our ability to think quick on our feet when our plans fall through.

This is the place where the ego begins to say, "But wait a minute! Aren't there really bad things in the world like rape, murder and disease?"

Absolutely! We cannot deny that rape, murder or disease are bad and most people would agree that peace, love and happiness are good. Yet because we have limited our conversation with these absolute labels, we have made little progress in diminishing the bad while increasing the good. In fact, the 20th century saw more mass murders than any other time in history because one group of people thought of another group as "the bad guys," an inferior race, an evil religion, or from the wrong country.

Whether we are talking about social dysfunctions or our own path to success, the solutions lie in the ability to think beyond the confines of labels.

If you are an entrepreneur, businessperson or other wealth seeker, the urge to judge things as good or bad can act like a cancer on your creativity. In fact, an increasing number of doctors of both conventional and alternative practices agree that anger, depression and other negative emotions that result from our compulsion to categorize events and people as good or bad are the root cause of cancer. And I am sure you want to avoid that!

So how can you eliminate this need to judge so that you can be open to creativity in your business?

Stick to the facts. What is it that you really mean when you say something is good or bad? Learn to elaborate on the meaning you really want to convey.

Children are continually told to "be good". When you stop to consider this phrase, you will realize that it is vague and rather void of meaning. It is simply a judgment -- a judgment that will shape the child's impression of himself. How should this child be good? Does this mean being polite, neat, quiet, keeping her hands to herself, eating all his dinner, putting the toilet seat down? What? There are many ways that a child can "be good", but he will never learn them without specifics.

Getting precise with your language by using more colorful and accurate descriptions is a good place to start. When you feel the urge to refer to something as good or bad, take a few extra seconds to rephrase the sentence to express the accurate description of what it is you really intend to communicate. It can be challenging to start this way, but in time it does get easier.

For example, if you get stuck in a traffic jam on your way to an important meeting, thinking "This sucks!" or "They're gonna kill me!" is of little use. However, if you approach it with the mindset of "This could be better." or "This is not where I want to be right now." Then you allow your brain to respond with thoughts of "Where do I want to be right now? How do I make that happen? Is there a back road I can take to get there? Can I phone in from the road? I'm probably not the only one stuck here." Chances are you will not only put your mind at ease, but you will find that whatever alternative you come up with is perfectly acceptable to the people with whom you planned to meet.

The truth is that the world is not black or white, red or blue, right or wrong, good or bad. It is far more interesting.

Looking back on my brief career as an actor many years ago, it is easy to see how stagnant my mindset was and how desperately I needed to reset it. I would continually flub my lines and throw my scene partners off by turning the line "What is it?" into "What's wrong?" In my limited world, any question or pause that someone would exhibit had to be the result of something going "wrong". So asking "What is wrong?" came naturally to me. In an attempt to make my lines roll off of my tongue effortlessly, I would slip into my typical way of perceiving the world.

Asking "What's wrong?", more often than not, prompts the responder to answer with drama such as "She ripped me off", "That guy's a jerk", or "This tastes like crap." Whereas "What is it?" is likely to get an answer that sticks more closely to the facts, "She gave me the wrong change", "That guy cut in front of me without warning" or "This tastes too sour." Of course this will depend upon the person with whom you are having the conversation and where his or her mindset is, but I think you can still understand the concept.

Name-calling is another way in which this tendency to judge the world manifests itself. Hey, I'll be honest, if someone get me angry, I'm just as likely to call them a scumbag as the next person. But, when I catch myself about to say something like this, I am actually attempting to describe something that I did not appreciate about their behavior, not the actual person. If you stop to think about this, it is probably true for you too.

When another person's actions anger us, it is because the ego perceives the action as something that diminishes our own sense of self-worth. Insults like scumbag, jerk or pig serve as a type of code for saying that a person is bad or did something to make you angry. While using such a label may make us feel superior to the other person, the inability to move past labeling makes it virtually impossible to learn how to deal with that person or at the least learn what could be a powerful lesson from our interaction with him or her.

In most cases, you will find that identifying the reasons why someone's actions or words upset you allows you to break free of emotional upset and make more grounded decisions. Was it a particular action? Did it bring up a bad childhood memory? Was it something that person said? Or the way they said it? Addressing the facts is key in avoiding the drama and finding solutions.

With practice, you will begin to forgive people for their actions as well. You start to notice that these people are simply unconscious victims of their own egos. When this happens, you develop an incredible sense of serenity that has a tremendous impact on your success. As Jesus said of the Roman soldiers who crucified him to the cross, "...forgive them, for they know not what they do." In other words, forgive them because they are unconscious.

You can learn to identify how judging gets in the way of progress by looking at the extreme views of any political issue. For example, when it comes to the environment, there are those who are willing to commit acts of terrorism to prevent a logging company from entering a forest. On the other end, there are those who would oppose any environmental legislation even when public health is at stake because they see it as an infringement on their rights. Both sides hold so tightly to their personal judgments of right and wrong that they are unable to reach any common ground. Both are unproductive and will only serve to keep the status quo instead of finding change that everybody can accept.

An interesting observation is that people in both camps (and this goes for any issue where there are such polar opposites) usually have a lot more in common where the core issue is concerned than they think. Both environmental advocates and detractors want "the best" for their children. Their respective understanding of what constitutes the best may be wildly different, but that very basic desire is often overshadowed by self-righteousness. It is also interesting to note that people on both sides of any issue often base their beliefs on well-intentioned, yet misguided facts or sometimes outright lies. The solution lies in the ability to drop the drama and come together to discuss the facts.

As you build your fortune, it would be helpful to begin thinking of how you can eliminate judgments and the resulting drama from your life. Sometimes you may feel as if the things that are getting in your way are completely uncontrollable. Maybe you have an overdue bill with no revenue to pay it or the deadline for some items you needed printed for an important meeting was missed. These may sound like impossible situations, but are they? Only if you allow them.

Being short on funds may prove to be an opportunity to find a partner whose skills complement your own so you can get more done faster or discover a freely available government grant to help you build your business. If your printer is behind schedule, perhaps you could find out if half of the job is done in time for your meeting. Chances are, you could get by just fine with less (business cards, posters or whatever) than you originally planned.

By changing the way you view an imperfect situation, you will become incredibly resourceful with an ability to adapt on the fly. Judging a situation as good or bad will not.

EXERCISE:

1. Read the newspaper with a critical eye or listen to the news with critical ear. There was a time when the media based its reporting on facts. Over the past 20 years ago, it would seem that those facts have become more and more skewed by the personal views of newscasters and reporters. What value judgments do they place on their stories? Are they labeling the people or causes they are reporting on? Do they call people names? It happens more often

than you think.

2. Ask yourself "What else is possible?", when you feel you reach what seems to be a dead end -- something that you may normally judge as being bad. Instead of seeing every hurdle as a brick wall, allow your brain to answer this simple question. Sit down in front of your computer or with a pad and paper and answer it. You will be amazed at how many alternatives you can find to a difficult or challenging situation. Your mind can be very creative if given the chance.

MORAL:

More often than not, judgment impairs the decision-making thereby increasing procrastination. Judgment also hampers creative thinking by processing the world as having only two states: good and bad, which eliminates your ability to see all the options in between. Letting go of the habit of judging others and yourself will unleash your greatest power to achieve. When you do this, NOTHING will be able to stand between you and success.

7 - The Separatist and The Joiner

"I'm not different for the sake of being different, for the desperate sake of being myself. I can't join your gang: you'd think I was a phony and I'd know it."
- Vivian Stanshall, musician

For some people, being accepted as normal by a group of peers is the most important element of life. They would bend over backwards to ensure their place amongst people whose lifestyle or attractiveness they admire.

Middle school and high school age kids are probably the best example of this. Somewhere just prior to the teen years, kids' egos really kick into high gear. Acceptance is an utmost priority and involves certain rites of passage such as choice of music, TV shows and clothes; whether or not they take drugs; what they can or cannot afford; what kinds of girls or boys they thing are cute and sexy; what their parents allow them to do -- date, watch R-rated movies, get piercings etc; and ultimately who their other friends are.

For others, the exact opposite is true. These individuals go out of their way whenever possible to demonstrate just how different they can be. Some even go so far as to turn themselves into "rejects" of society such as someone who tattoos every inch of their body, a woman who shaves her head and even criminals.* Even some people who say they are gay only call themselves so out of the "novelty" and attention they feel it brings them.

At first glance, it would seem that these two types of people are very different. When closely analyzed, however, these two types of people operate from the same desire -- to be recognized for something. Many times, it does not even matter if the attention is positive or negative.

We all succumb to seek acceptance either for being different or the same. In many ways, we experience both simultaneously.

Although they often like to consider themselves misfits of society, "rebels", for example, often like to hang out with other like-minded people whom they deem to be cool. (Yeah, I know that's the nerdiest way to say that!) By the same token, more "mainstream" people who base what is acceptable by what they see on TV or in trendy magazines would not be caught dead wearing the same outfit as another member of their clique to the office or at a wedding.

This desire to be the same, different or some combination of the two seems harmless enough, but for many people, it is an underlying dysfunction that overrides rational decision-making.

I think it is not uncommon for someone to give up an opportunity because they fear that their friends will look down upon them for that decision. Many years ago a friend of mine told me she would never go to Hawaii because of the injustices she perceived the U.S. government to have inflicted upon the native Hawaiians. Years later when I got the chance to visit Hawaii I was afraid to tell her for fear that I would be berated for my decision. In the end, I decided that if she was going to attack me or no longer consider me a friend because of my trip, then she was simply not the kind of friend I would want in my life anyway. Nobody wants to walk on eggshells with their friends!

To my surprise, she said "Another friend of mine just moved there. She said it's wonderful. I can't wait to have enough money to go!" What the ___? Are you serious? This is the same woman who would go on hour-long rants about how she would never go there. Now she was ready to pack her bags.

Now, I did not base my travel decision on her personal convictions (which obviously had been overturned during the course of a year), but do not think that others would not have.

One very close member of my family is this way. At almost 50 years old, she makes nearly all of her decisions on what her friends suggest. This includes everything from her favorite TV shows to the latest health fads.

I remember when Seinfeld was a popular TV show here in the United States. One night I turned it on while she was over. She said she had heard people at work saying that they liked it and then proceeded to talk throughout the entire episode, not even letting up for a second. As soon as the show was over, she said "That was stupid. It wasn't even funny." Two months later we were talking and she said, "Did you see Seinfeld last night? That's my favorite show!" What do you think happened? That's right. She was at her friend's house sometime during that two-month period and watched the show in the presence of a friend whose opinion she valued. While with me she has always had a need to show how different we are, with this friend she has always had a need to gain approval.

Can you imagine how many opportunities must pass her by because she can only like or dislike based upon the decisions of others? In many ways, she is very successful. She has a lot of money, a nice car and a big house. Much of this is because her friends come from wealthy families, so you could say that her association with wealthy people has paid off. Nonetheless, for whatever reason, she feels she cannot make a move without the blessings of her friends.

Unfortunately, most of us probably do not have the opportunity to hang out with many wealthy people, so seeking this type of validation from people who are broke is far worse if our goal is financial success.

Seeking the approval of others is indeed very "childish" behavior, but it is certainly not uncommon for the ego to express itself in such a way. As much as I hate to admit it, I frequently demonstrated this type of behavior until about the age of 30. It was not until I realized how fickle people could be that I began caring less and less about what others thought about me.

I got sick of people leaving me hanging holding onto their ideas of right, wrong and what is acceptable only to find out that their convictions were not as strong as they purported. Now, as much as possible, I try to stick to what makes me happy and fulfilled. Life is too short to let others be the boss of me. I suspect you feel the same way about your life too.

EXERCISE:

Make a list of things you think make you different from your friends. Now determine which things you think your friends would ridicule you for if they knew about them. They may know about some things, but not others.

Next, make a list of things that you share in common with your friends. Are these truly things you have in common? Or have you adapted your likes and dislikes to align with other people's assessment of the world?

Then you must decide for yourself, do you want to pretend to be someone you are not to hold on to a friendship? This may "work" for you, in which case, I would not suggest you change anything. However, if what works for you on one level stands between you and success, you must figure out how to make the two co-exist harmoniously or give up one until the conditions are right for achieving both.

MORAL:

Be true to yourself. It is fine to have friends who have different interests. Clearly you will both share some very similar core values, but do not let their choices dictate your actions.

8 - The Confidant(e)

"Boldness be my friend." - William Shakespeare

A big mistake I think we all make is telling our friends and family about our pie in the sky plans for making more money or otherwise becoming independently wealthy. Some are happy for us, but others are jealous. In both cases, however, they probably do not have much faith in our ability to achieve a level of success that has always seemed to allude them.

Friends or family who discourage you do so because of limitations in their own thinking. Those of us who have grown up in a Puritanical culture such as we have here in the U.S., have likely been taught not to think of ourselves as being particularly special or deserving of wealth or freedoms that are intended for a few special or privileged individuals. For crying out loud, who do you think you are to dream so big?

Remember that just because your friend or family member does not think that he or she can create great wealth, does not mean that you cannot. They are entitled to their opinions, but that does not mean that you have to succumb to them.

On the other hand, you may have people in your circle that are in awe of what you do. They admire your ambition, but they do not quite understand basic concepts or steps involved in creating true wealth.

These people will often put ideas in your head that make you think that you are shooting too high. As a result, you begin to second guess yourself and readjust your goals.

Unfortunately, when your goals become unclear, you lose focus and can no longer see the target toward which you are aiming.

Many people suffer from a scarcity mindset, meaning that they remain stuck in the concept that there is not enough wealth to go around and if there is, that everyone and their mother is out to get a part of it so you might as well not even try.

Recently, I was speaking to a friend, who coincidentally is living off of her husband's inheritance, about my business. While on the one hand she is very excited that I have such lofty goals, she simply does not understand that working online does not mean working 80-hour weeks. She kept asking questions about what my online competition is like and how I could work so many hours away from my children.

I quickly realized that these are her limitations, which should not be my concern. She simply does not understand that online work does not need to be the same as a full-time job working for someone else. The concept of automated income is completely foreign to her.

So if you feel that others' opinions will get you off track, then avoid talking to them about your plans. You may even want to limit your exposure to such people for a time.

When people are in a scarcity mindset, it is often reflected in every area of their lives. They will constantly complain of not having enough money for food and housing. They curse the rich for stealing their way to the top. Interestingly enough, they also tend to buy things they will never use or cannot afford to give themselves a false sense of abundance. These items often have no inherent value to them except that they perceive them as items that will win them favor in the eyes of their peers.

You do not want that kind of energy seeping into your subconscious. If you cannot limit your exposure to those individuals, then at least try to change the conversation every time they hurl another downer at you.

Remember that whether you think you can achieve something or you think you cannot, you are right. But would you rather those thoughts for better or for worse be your own thoughts or those of the people around you?

Recently, I was listening to a recording of a popular life coach and had an a-ha moment. She said that of the thousands of thoughts we have on any given day, only a handful are truly our own. The rest are a combination of familiar phrases and negative feedback we have heard from others throughout our lives. What a concept!

When you set some lofty goal for yourself, do you hear a nagging or even more subtle voice saying "You can't do that.", "You'll be working for the rest of your life.", "That'll never happen." What she suggests is that every time you hear that negative self-talk to ask yourself out loud "Whose idea is that?" By asking yourself this question repeatedly, your subconscious begins to realize that so many of the phrases that get repeated in your head have nothing to do with your reality.

Do this consecutively for three days and I can guarantee that your mind will begin to open up to many opportunities and choices you can make in your journey to financial success.

EXERCISE:

1. Make a list of your ideal wealth generation strategies. Describe everything about them including:

    - how many hours you want to work in it

    - what methods you will use to generate income

    - how much money you intend to make daily (often an easier target to wrap your brain around than saying a million dollars per year)

    - things you will do with your newfound wealth and time.

    Keep this list handy or, better yet, post the list on a wall near your bed and/or in your office where you will see it frequently to help embed those ideas deep down in your subconscious.

2. Keep asking yourself "Whose idea is that?" every time you hear a negative voice in your head. Do not expect an answer most times. However, recognize that these ideas are not yours, but they belong to someone else. I cannot begin to tell you how powerful I have found this exercise.

MORAL:

The bottom line here is not to allow your friend's and family's baggage to become your own. You *must* know that the sky has no limit. If they do not get it right now, that's OK. When you start living the four-hour work week, they will all come out of the woodwork to find out how you are doing it.

9 - The Pauper

"Being rich is a good thing. Not just in the obvious sense of benefitting you and your family, but in the broader sense. Profits are not a zero sum game. The more you make, the more of a financial impact you can have."
- Mark Cuban, businessman

Another holdover from our Puritanical culture is the concept of rich men (or women as the case may be) as some sort of abomination in the eyes of God. How many times have we heard rich people cursed for being too greedy or selfish? What about sayings like "the rich just get richer" or "money is the root of all evil"? Did you ever catch yourself saying "Well, if I had that kind of money, I'd give most of it to charity (a relative, friend or other person in need)" ?

This kind of thinking is ingrained in Western culture, mainly through misinterpretation of Scripture. In the book of Matthew, a young rich man asks Jesus which good deeds are rewarded with eternal life. Jesus replies that one must obey the Commandments.

After noting that he is already observant of the Commandments, the rich man asks, "What do I still lack?" To which Jesus answers, "If you want to be perfect, go, sell your possessions and give to the poor, and you will have treasure in heaven. Then come, follow me."

Upon hearing this, the rich man unhappily leaves suggesting that he has no intention of giving up his wealth to follow Jesus. At which point Jesus utters to his disciples, "I tell you the truth, it is hard for a rich man to enter the kingdom of heaven. Again I tell you, it is easier for a camel to go through the eye of a needle than for a rich man to enter the kingdom of God."

At face value it seems that God does not approve of rich people. Most scholars however believe that what he was in fact saying is that the riches of this earth do not exist in the afterlife. In other words, you can't take it with you.

To think about it in another way, what kind of God wants people to worry, suffer and starve on a daily basis? Not mine! My God wants me to be abundant and happy.

To me, it is ludicrous that as a society we have collectively allowed the ego to tell us that God (fate or whatever force we believe in) does not want us to be happy and affluent. However, we gladly accept that Satan is the root of being joyful and rich. Don't believe me? Again, let me illustrate.

Over the past decade, I have learned a powerful energy medicine technique that uses a series of tapping on acupressure points to get rid of pain, negative emotions and illness within seconds. I used it on both friends and clients who had been suffering with various health issues for years -- issues that had not responded to the most invasive conventional medical techniques.

Most people were fascinated by how rapidly they became pain-free and profusely thanked me for my services. Others jokingly called me a witch and reported that their problems never returned.

There was a small segment of people, however, who saw the practice as Satanic. One woman who was immediately cured of hot flashes reported "When I saw how quickly my pain subsided, I realized that this was from the Devil." As a nurse, she was completely fine with pumping her body full of chemicals and dangerous drugs regardless of the outcome, yet a simple technique which worked and made her body function properly without disturbing any other systems in the body was "from the Devil".

Seriously?? The Devil wants you effortlessly pain-free, but God wants you to have an arduous uphill battle involving body-destroying therapies? It may sound crazy, but think of how we apply this same logic to money.

In our culture, are we not able to do a lot more for others if we have sufficient money to donate or at least to free us up enough to offer our time for worthy causes? Yet we allow ourselves to become so turned off by wealth that we have even carried our distaste for the rich over to what we eat. How often have you heard someone feel shameful over eating something that was "too rich"? How often have you elected to eat an insipid piece of cardboard for dinner instead of eating a "rich" and satisfying steak, quiche or something laced in a fine cream sauce because the latter is "sinful"?[2]

The truth is, your brain does not know if you are eschewing rich food or a rich you. So choose your words carefully.

---

[2] As a nutritionist, I cannot let it go without saying that eating any of these rich foods are not the minefield the low-fat establishment would have you believe. In fact, quite the opposite is true.

Indeed, many rich people are greedy and selfish. There are also many rich people who lie, cheat and steal their way to the top. But get this. There are just as many poor people who take the same entitled approach to life. They may not get as far financially, but it is not for the lack of trying. No matter the person, it is the decision of individuals, not a rule that proceeds wealth. It is their limited understanding of true wealth that makes these types of people feel that deceit is the only way to get ahead. We cannot allow the choices of others to stand in the way of how we go about business.

It feels good to the ego to denigrate someone over their successes (or feeling smart for eating "sensibly") as much as it does to think oneself capable of making wiser and more compassionate decisions with the same amounts of money. Unfortunately, this does us little good when we set out on a quest to achieve financial freedom.

If we cannot feel good for someone else's successes, then why on earth would we want to join their ranks? After all, most people like to be liked. So if we cannot rejoice in someone else's successes, then how can we comfortably become financially successful ourselves?

If we continue to think negatively about wealth, what happens if we ourselves should hit our targets? GUILT! We feel that we do not deserve it. We think that we should somehow offer it up to others.

This is one major reason that so many lottery winners end up squandering their winnings and end up in debt. Their inner being is uncomfortable with possessing that much money. The cure to this is changing your inner dialogue.

In fact, recently I saw a man buy about $20 worth of lottery tickets in the local convenience store. It seemed to be a part of his weekly routine.

As he was paying the cashier he kept uttering, "It's not like I'm gonna win. My body likes working 102 hour weeks." This man was either addicted to the status quo, was saying this as code for "I'm really a good person" or in typical working class fashion held disdain for rich people. No matter how you look at it, he was doing himself a disservice.

All I could think was "Wow! I'm glad I'm not stuck in that kind of thinking!" I cannot imagine how unfulfilling my life would be today if I was just going through the motions like this guy. My online business grows steadily every day and that could not happen without the faith that money will flow to me more easily as time goes on.

Internationally renowned life coach, Morgana Rae, shares a great story of her unique solution to her own history of financial struggle. Early in her coaching career, she had a shameful secret -- she could not even pay her rent. Even as she was guiding clients to land television series and sell films, she had an uncanny ability to repel money in her own life.

Popular programs on mindset, magnetism, or marketing were of no help. She was following all the recommendations properly, but the results were dismal. That is when she decided to find her own solution by making money her next area of spiritual growth. This is when she uncovered her own hidden relationship with money in a way that no other teacher had taught -- a personal, living, breathing relationship with money.

By drawing on her darkest experiences, she was able to discover her unexpected, unconscious reasons for protecting herself from money. Her ego had turned money into a monster. By recognizing this "money monster", she was then able to apply her own process of Alchemy to transmute those obstacles into the foundation of money magnetism. She made money "fall in love" with her. The very next day she signed four new clients at double the highest rate she had ever charged. That was genesis of a whole new approach to wealth coaching.

As of today, Morgana has gone on to guide hundreds of thousands of people worldwide in making money fall in love with them too and is one of the most successful and respected coaches in personal development. She earns more in an hour than she used to make in a year, by helping more people than she ever imagined possible.

EXERCISE:

Surround yourself with things and experiences you would like to have or do when you are rich. You are taking baby steps here, so do not go out and spend money you do not have yet. Garage sales and discount stores (such as HomeGoods or Marshalls here in the U.S.) can be a source of some very, very good buys. Online discount sites like Gilt or Groupon can also bring a touch of luxury to your life at a huge discount.

Note that these should be items that you are truly drawn to, not just clutter that you will purchase to stockpile in some area of your home in an attempt to impress somebody else.

Like me, you will likely find that as your income goes up, your need for knickknacks and even a wide variety of essentials such as clothing and shoes goes down.

For most people, there is no need to wait to start living the good life. Start now and get used to it. And when people compliment your high-end possessions, resist the temptation to be apologetic and explain that you got it on sale. Instead, politely say "Thank you!" treating it like it is completely normal because in fact it is.

By the way, if by chance, you get wind of someone calling you stuck up because you can do and have things they cannot, REJOICE! Yes, this is a huge milestone! At this point you know you are headed in the right direction because someone cares enough about your accomplishments to think about what you are doing. They are in effect putting more energy into YOU!

The next time you hear of another person becoming an instant millionaire, instead of cursing that person for not having to work for it or having an edge in one way or another, think to yourself "Good for him (or her, as the case may be)!" Be sincere about it. This will make your subconscious more comfortable with the idea of having more than enough money for your basic daily needs being a good thing that is alright to have. With practice, this technique will gradually move you closer to joining the ranks of other independently well off people around the globe.

Morgana Rae has designed a workbook about manifesting money using her financial alchemy method. It is an easy step-by-step journey through changing your relationship with money. A must-read for anyone serious about making money while remaining true to themselves. Check the resources section for more information.

MORAL:

There is nothing bad about being wealthy or just plain old rich. Embrace it, know you are worthy and make it happen.

10 - The Tycoon-In-Training

"The hardest thing to understand in the world is the income tax."
- Albert Einstein

Many people set out to make millions when they want financial stability. But to the average Joe a million dollars is really difficult to visualize. Yeah, it would be a lot, but how much? A pallet's worth of singles, fives or hundred dollar bills? I think you get the idea.

So let's back up. Think of what five dollars looks like in your hand. You probably have a five somewhere within reach right now. That is much easier to understand, right? Can you visualize 20 fives in your hand? Yes, also pretty easy, right? If so, then this is where you need to start.

Focus on the familiar then replicate those processes to allow it to multiply.

If you have followed any law of attraction or motivational teachers, you have heard it before: visualization is a powerful tool. If you set out to make a certain amount of money, then you must be able to connect with what that amount of money translates to in your brain. If your brain cannot see it, it will be much harder to attain.

Seeing that money in your mind's eye, however, is only part of the equation. The other component is making that money mean some thing to you.

Throughout my life, I have observed people gladly shell out thousands of dollars on crap products and feel ashamed to ask for their money back. I have seen others spend money on excellent products, which they have never put to use. And I have seen people beg for free trials of two dollar items.

All of these scenarios amount to the same thing. These people have a much stronger connection to two or five dollars than they do to $1,500 or $10,000. And if someone cannot even imagine what as little as $1,500 is like in their hands, how on earth can they make a connection to a million?

Rich people and those seriously planning to get rich, however, will usually demand to get their money's worth over virtually any amount of money. If they are going to write off a loss, you can bet it would be the lower amount of money, not the higher amount.

During my first attempt to learn Internet marketing, I spent $6,000 on a teleclass that was complete nonsense. It was 23 weeks long and offered zero value to anyone who participated. The people in this class cursed the course creator. Many agreed that much cheaper courses they had bought were far more helpful, but I was the ONLY one to ask for her money back.

A few months later, when I was talking to some women from the same class, I mentioned a six-dollar per month computer program that interfaced with Facebook. Nearly all of these women got hot under the collar about how it was a *scam* and a *rip off*. They were terrified of laying out a six dollar per month investment! Do you see how backwards this type of thinking is?

I have long since lost touch with many of those women, but as far as I know, I am now the only one making decent money with automated online income streams, which is what we all set out to do when we met. Meanwhile the ones I have kept in contact with have all gone back to their J-O-Bs.

One last concept I must mention regarding money is that while you might like to think that having a million dollars is your ultimate goal, you would probably be able to thrive and live the type of lifestyle you want on far less than that. In *The Four-Hour Work Week*, Tim Ferriss refers to people in this situation as the New Rich (NR).

He cites several examples of people who have sold an invention, company or investment property as well as those who run automated Internet companies so that they can live off of the proceeds. In some cases, these individuals choose to live in parts of the world where the cost of living is significantly lower so that they can live a very cushy life without the overhead of living in a first world country.

Think about this as a possible option for you.

EXERCISE:

I learned this exercise from Esther and Jerry Hicks's book *Ask and It Is Given*. Grab an old checkbook that you no longer use. Every day for a month, write a check for an expensive item you would like. Do this in increments. So, for example, on the first day, write a check for $1,000 and make it out to whatever place you would like for a specific item. In my case, I might buy a nice piece of high end luggage I have had my eye on.

The next day, increase the amount to $2,000. And write a check for an item that fits that bill, like a nice $2,000 watch. The following day, spend $3,000 etc.

Rules: Try to stick to stuff that will be fun or bring you enjoyment. Do not carry over money you do not spend one day over to the next night. You must spend the entire amount of money each day.

By the end of the month, you will have $30,000 to spend in one day. This sounds easy, but it gets hard when you are trying to determine what would cost you roughly $27,000 and then to follow it up the following day with another purchase for $28,000.

Spending money can be somewhat exhausting when done in this fashion, which is why I suggest focusing on only one month, but you could keep doing this for an entire year or more as the Hicks recommend. How much money would you have then???

MORAL:

The take home message here is to make ALL of your investments count, but especially the ones demanding a huge outlay of money. Do not let anyone take your hard-earned cash, if they have not earned the right by delivering you value. Many people become millionaires simply by saving or spending money more judiciously than others. Let your money know you care about it and you will be entrusted to handle more of it.

11 - The Cynic

"Trust in dreams, for in them is hidden the gate to eternity."
- Khalil Gibran

While improving your connection to physical money is one way to draw more of it to you, like many people, you may still struggle with making visuals work for you. Many law of attraction gurus will suggest that you cut out pictures of a vacation you want to take or the new car you will buy with your newfound riches, but these pictures may not offer you the deeper connection you need to reach those goals.

What I have consistently found is that stating what you want in the affirmative as if you already have achieved it does wonders to make the earth move in directions you never thought possible just so that your dreams can come true.

The practice of meditation is a testament to the mind's ability to create the reality it wants internally (peace, relaxation), but did you know that meditation can also create the outer reality your mind seeks as well? Part of the reason this happens is because once you become in tune to what it is like to actually have those things you desire, your mind moves into a state of creativity to put you in the right place at the right time.

One very memorable example in my own life was when I needed to graduate college and had only one semester to finish. I had already been living on my own in New York City for a few years earning a measly four dollars per hour plus occasional tiny commissions working for a French newspaper. The only solution I could come up with for paying this last semester of college was to put it on my credit card. This was incredibly hard for me because I never liked paying for something up front on my credit card if I did not already have the money in the bank. Paying $400 per month in rent, I was already struggling just to keep the minimum balance in my bank account.

As I handed my credit card over to the school official for payment, I remember thinking to myself that the money would have to come soon. After that, I really did not give the statement another thought.

About a week after paying for school, I had a falling out with my boss, which prompted me to look for another job. I went on two interviews. And was offered a job which paid $27,000 per year. Not bad back in the early 1990s for someone not even out of college and with no real skills in the job she was about to take on. With this job, I was able to pay down my credit card within three months, move to a nicer apartment and still had enough money to travel around Europe for two weeks after graduation.

A good friend of mine, named Kris, had a somewhat similar experience. For years she tried to micromanage the Universe to deal with the emotional pain of her childhood. She tried everything from Atheism to Paganism to find answers to her pain. The result was erratic behavior and further pain, which culminated in a hasty marriage, abusive relationship and eventually divorce.

One night, just after her husband had left her, she broke down and offered herself up to God begging for a way out of her mess. As she put it, she did not even do it in the "nicest way". She basically said, "God, I made a mess of my life. Fix it."

At the time she was being evicted from her apartment, but the very day after making this plea, an apartment was offered to her by an acquaintance she ran into on the street as she walked to work. Shortly after that, she was offered weekly counseling at a super-reduced rate of only $10 per session. Even though she often could not come up with the $10 most weeks, this woman continued to see her for the next 10 years.

Throughout her life, she had approached life from a mental place. A place of controlling what she felt did not work. Everything she did not like about her life was someone else's fault -- her parents, her husband, her body, etc. The problem with trying to control her life was that her imagination was not as creative and expansive as that of the Universe. So while she attempted to make intellectual changes to her life, she could not foresee the limitations of what she was manifesting. However, once she let go of control, the Universe (or God, if you prefer) found a way to make things right.

I cannot say that things turned around 100% overnight. She did not find a check for $1 million in the mail the next day, but her life is 180 degrees from where it was 20 years ago. She is currently a homeowner (something she did completely on her own), is a spiritual counselor and has now been in a loving, committed relationship for the past several years. She is living proof that when you surrender and trust in the Universe, all things are possible.

Remember that your current circumstances do not dictate where you will be in 20 years, 5 years or even one hour from now as long as you are taking consistent action. Go through life as if tomorrow will be a better day. Offer up to the Universe what you cannot handle and a way will be made.

It is a lack of trust in the universe that leads us to get trapped by our own thoughts of scarcity. Despite the fact that there are many billionaires walking the planet, we subconsciously believe that there is not enough money for us to attain our fortunes as well. As a result, we become miserly, never realizing that we have to open our hands to receive money as well as to spend it.

This is precisely why even though most people recognize that contributing money to those who are less fortunate is a powerful way to increase their own wealth, they rarely, if ever, do it. Some cover up their lack of participation by saying that they want to make sure the money is actually getting to the people who need it and not getting lost in some bureaucratic system. Understandable, but researching various organizations should turn up at least one worthy cause.

Who says donations should go through large organizations? On the local level there are soup kitchens and shelters that do wonderful work for individuals right in our own neighborhoods. Many people have relatives who have fallen on hard times or who live in a third world country that could use the money.

If we are serious about creating prosperity, we must not hide behind excuses, but be proactive in every way including trusting the universe to provide enough for us as well as others and to help where we can.

EXERCISE:

Learn to trust that the universe will meet you part way. Start with something small. Tell the universe that the next time you drive up to the mall, you will get a parking spot in front of the location where you want to park; that you will find the money for a much needed vacation; or that all of your important tasks will get done by the end of the day.

The key here is not to over think it and try to bully the universe into meeting your demands, but to go about your work in a purposeful way knowing that the light is at the end of the tunnel.

You may think that you worked out the perfect scenario for how the future will take shape, but know that the universe does indeed work in mysterious ways. Sometimes the universe may throw you a curve ball by sending a potential disaster your way, but a temporary setback may be masking your golden egg on the other side.

Sometimes it takes a while to get into the groove of asking and receiving, but when you are in the zone and performing the tasks you need to move you forward, the universe has a way of making your job easier.

MORAL:

At the risk of sounding new agey, I must stress that once you connect with an idea, the universe will move mountains to make it reality. All you have to do is dream it and then find a way to make it feel as if it is really happening.

If you want to travel with the money that is coming to you, then start collecting travel gear or other items that make you feel like you are getting on a plane tomorrow. If you have your eye on a new car that you would not be able to afford without a cash reserve in the bank, then get something you would want to use in your new car. If you want to be successful in your line of work, make friends with people who are already succeeding in that area (try finding them on Facebook)!

This is not a license to simply make a wish and then sit around the house watching TV and drinking beer all day. Like with the lottery, "you have to be in it to win it". So remember to always take some sort of action toward your goals while maintaining the faith that things will take shape in your favor.

Whatever it is you have your heart set on, just know deep in your heart that it is as good as yours now and soon enough it will be.

12 - The Multi-Tasker

"Multi-tasking arises out of distraction itself."
- Marilyn vos Savant, writer

One thing that I struggle with frequently and see others fall prey to is getting distracted by little annoyances, things that have little or nothing to do with a task previously identified as a priority, yet they become an obsessive point of focus. Let me explain.

Let's say you decide you are going to try out a new software to increase your productivity. This software is supposed to be super easy to use and can be implemented in a matter of 15 minutes or less. You launch the program, watch the 10-minute tutorial and 90 minutes later you realize that you still cannot get the darn thing to perform as promised.

Now would it not have been much better to time yourself for 15 minutes and then email customer support about the issue you are experiencing? After all, you are just testing out the software at this stage, it is not an integral part of your work. Once you put out a ticket to the support desk, just write a note reminding yourself to get in touch with them later on in the week.

The ego is a master of obsessive-compulsive disorders. Remember, it will do anything to ensure its survival. And distracting you from your goals with something that it can later use as an excuse for not reaching your goals guarantees the important role it believes it plays in your life.

We see this time and again in politics. Politicians love to make promises about making their neighborhoods or countries better for its citizens by providing jobs, social programs, and putting more money into everybody's pockets. However, when it comes down to responsible voting to make these things happen, they bicker about minute details in an effort to make the opposing political parties look bad.

So instead of getting the most important bills passed so that citizens can begin reaping rewards, they stall and waste unfathomable amounts of money on petty arguments. In 2010, for example, the U.S. Congress spent upwards of $2.6 million on bottled water, food and snacks during numerous meetings supposedly aimed at resolving the current economic crisis. This money could have be used in part to repair schools and roads or put more policemen on the streets in high crime areas -- all efforts that would have provided more jobs.

The obsession over minutiae, which in many cases is simply "getting my way", overshadows the greater good of doing the job they were elected to do.

Another place where I see this type of behavior is in the holistic community. I have been a member of various holistic-minded communities for nearly 20 years.

Many people in these communities take a very "anti-" stance to life. They are anti-greed, anti-corporate enterprise, and anti-conventional medicine to name a few.

The trend in these groups is to talk about supporting small local businesses, be it a farm that grows food for the community or an alternative healthcare practitioner. Now here is the kicker: They often expect the local farm or alternative healthcare practitioner to give away their products for next to nothing, if not for free. Even worse, many people working in services that cater to this community are afraid to request fair wages for their work.

It's true. As a holistic nutritionist, I have had people in these communities tell me that they did not want to pay my rates even though they know that what I do works only to pay twice as much to a conventional doctor who made their health situation much worse.

Likewise, a friend who runs a food-buying club in her community is often begged to front the bill for members, who then brag to her about brand new jewelry or other non-essential items they recently bought for themselves.

And finally, the service provider in this community who does not make a fair living wage ends up shopping at places like Wal-Mart, often cited as the epitome of greedy corporations for these types of groups.

So in this case, people become so blinded with anger as well as obsessed at the thought of going against things they would like to see changed that they end up back at square one being part of the problem instead of part of the solution. They, too, completely miss their goals.

A fellow Internet marketer, Chris Diamond, recently shared his story of how focusing turned his business around.

Chris became interested in the topic of getting focused and busyness after noticing that he was not getting much done in either his personal or business life. He was very messy and disorganized. When someone is surrounded by clutter, the same disorganization is present in the mind. This state of disorganization made him constantly overwhelmed by the fact that he just was not getting anything done.

He had created so many business projects, that he had trouble focusing on one thing in particular. It only got worse by the fact that he was constantly chasing the next big trend in Internet marketing. It drove him crazy.

It was not until he made a conscious decision to get more focused and concentrate on one project at a time until they were completed that he began to see successes. It was about that time that he built the website doubletimetoday.com.

Chris believes that when you "single focus" instead of allowing your attention to be diverted by different projects, you get too easily distracted to the point that you cannot get anything completed.

He suggests that we should work in one-hour uninterrupted chunks of time to get things done faster as discipline is developed through patience, passion and having a sense of purpose. Combining all three allow you to stay on top of your projects until they are completed.

Lastly, he suggests to know why you are in business. Is there something you want to avoid in order to get things done? The more reasons you come up with, the stronger discipline you will develop to endure the failures and setbacks along the way to see your way through to success.

EXERCISE:

Think about your cause. Almost everybody has one. What is it you would like to see different about the world around you?

Now on a piece of paper write down all the ways in which advocating for this issue will impact your future. Will it mean that you will get ahead by keeping someone else down? Or will it simply mean more respect amongst your peers? Or perhaps it will mean absolutely nothing at all. Be completely honest with yourself. Keep writing for at least 30 minutes. There are often more than one or two justifications (read: excuses) that will come to mind.

Hopefully after completing this exercise you will realize that these excuses do little more than distract you from your bigger goals. As a side benefit, I am hoping that by putting this into perspective you begin to realize just how much power you have to make things happen for you, not to you.

MORAL:

Live in a state of awareness by taking note of your thoughts and actions. When you are aware of what you think and do, your ego cannot get the best of you by taking you off course.

Whenever you feel yourself getting wrapped up in some sort of conflict or difficult moment, decide whether or not it is worth your time. Is it distracting you from your big goal? What is the worst that would happen if you leave it alone and continue working on your mission? Is there a temporary solution that would enable you to stay focused? If it is not worth sacrificing your financial goal, then leave it alone and move on.

Do not get entangled in non-relevant issues you really do not need to get personally invested in. Do not let your ego get the best of you by distracting you from your goals!

13 - The Old Fuddy-Duddy

"The Internet is the Viagra of big business."
- Jack Welch, businessman

Although Internet marketers should know this, I believe that many would-be entrepreneurs and future millionaires fail to reach their goals because they do not realize how vast the freaking Internet is! Just like my friend who worried about how many other people are promoting products online, many people who dream of a better financial future get sucked into worrying about saturation and competition. It Is called the World Wide Web for a reason. Because people all over the planet have access to it!

That means that you no longer need to walk around handing out a stack of business cards, attending local meetings or making cold calls. You could still include it in your promotional methods, but you now have the potential of reaching your audience anywhere across the globe.

Let that sink in.

OK. Now if you still cannot wrap your brain around this concept, then think of it this way.

There are more than 1.3 billion people living in the People's Republic of China. That's BILLION with a "B"! And there are millions more Chinese living all around the world. In fact, I cannot recall the last time that I have gone anywhere in the world, be it big city or small town where I did not run into at least a handful of Chinese people. Chances are, you have experienced the same thing. And that's just one group of people!

What I'm trying to get at here is that there are an unimaginable number of people in just one country, but that number is not even representative of the entire population across the planet. There are also many people, like me, who can trace part of their family tree back to China as well.

Add another 5 billion to that number and now you have the entire planet's population and a huge chunk of that population has access to a computer. Over 750 million of them alone are Facebook users. These numbers boggle the mind, but I think they really illustrate just how enormous the Internet is and how much opportunity is out there.

Just like with the million dollar example earlier, it is hard for most people to wrap their brains around this concept.

As for competition, you must realize that for every person who attempts to make a living from the Internet, there are hundreds of thousands more who think of the Internet as a place to get free information and chat with friends on social networks. Sure, they know that sites such as Amazon and Ebay exist to making money, but they have no idea that most of the ads they see and the links on websites actually generate income for average people just like you and me.

In recent years, I have seen many local businesses including contractors go out of business. Why? Because they insisted on doing things the old school way. They only take checks instead of credit cards, they will not put up a website and many of them do not even have any system of automated payments set up.

Like it or not, the Internet is here to stay. If you want to build a successful business today, with little exception, you need some sort of presence on the Internet -- whether on your site or another large site like Angie's List or Amazon. If possible (and it is really easy), you should be set up to receive automatic payments on your website.

Don't allow your ego to get the best of you by refusing to move with the times. Find out what your mental blocks are and fix them. This could be financial life or death for your business.

Think about the potential that the Internet brings to you to be able to make money in any number of ways -- even while you sleep! The numbers are astounding! To me, there is no better feeling than opening my email to find that I have made a sale (or twenty) from several different websites. Making money on the Internet is addictive.

EXERCISES:

1. Study people's faces. It does not matter where you are: at your kid's school, in an airport, shopping mall, wherever. Just look at faces and study their complexity. Notice how we all, for the most part, have the same features – eyes, nose, mouth, ears, but none of them are quite the same. The more you look at each individual as being just that, the more you realize how many needs there are to be satisfied. After all, if they look so different on the outside, they must have different needs, wants and desires on the inside, no?

2. Walk through a bookstore or magazine shop, or visit Amazon.com. Notice the wide array of books and magazines with differing views, ideas and hobbies. Each book or magazine represents another idea

around which you can build your business. If you have been struggling to get a money-making idea, this is a great place to start brainstorming. This becomes even more powerful when you consider the potential that opens up once you delve deeper into your own spin on these different views and ideas.

MORAL:

It is a big, big world we live in. There is always room for another voice and another idea, so why not your voice and your idea? Whether you choose to start a traditional brick and mortar business, invent a product, offer a service, make a movie or write a book, you need a web presence. Do not limit yourself to a local audience.

14 - The Workaholic

"If you tell the truth, you don't have to remember anything." - Mark Twain

If you are like me, then being rich means working less hours, not more. But every once in a while, you find yourself working well over the average 40 hours per week that you may have had in your regular job. There are many reasons for this.

1. Many people, especially Americans, have had it shoved down their throats from birth that the only honest day's work involves "working your fingers to the bone". It Is all part of the "no pain, no gain" philosophy. As a result, finding a comfortable living without doing much seems somehow like cheating or even forbidden. As a nation, we have become addicted to work and take less vacation than virtually

everyone on the planet.

2. You might feel guilty about making money easily while your friends struggle to make ends meet. The knowledge you have is simply not part of their consciousness. That is not your fault. It Is just a reality.

3. For some people the struggle gives them (really their egos) a sense of purpose. If they did not have their finances and hardships to complain about, they would feel a void. Do not be one of those people.

4. You panic because deep down inside you do not believe that making money can be as simple as setting up automated money-generating systems or selling an invention. How many times have you looked for an item, maybe your keys or glasses, for hours only to find out that they were right under your nose the whole time? This happens because you panic that you may never find them. So instead of being centered and retracing your steps, you allow your mind to become distracted by negative thoughts. Making money can be the same. Just set up simple systems and do not approach it with panic, otherwise you will begin spinning your wheels and never be able to get your business off the ground.

5. Working for yourself in an unconventional capacity can be lonely. If you cannot find someone in your family or circle of friends to support you or be able to chat with about your new business, then it can get discouraging quickly. Do your best to find a business partner, a friend on an online forum or a mentor to follow. Having someone to discuss ideas with or keep you accountable can really help you move forward by keeping you on task and excited about

what you are achieving.

6. If part of your stumbling comes from inexperience in running a business, I would highly suggest joining a support forum. At first, I did not think it was something that pertained to me, but once I got inside, I realized just how powerful being part of a supportive community is.

7. Being busy is yet another way in which the ego establishes importance to ensure its own survival. In fact, you may find yourself frequently creating new tasks for yourself when in fact you could delegate that work to someone else – a spouse, child or an assistant. Being busy can be good. Just make sure that you are busy with things that are useful to your business, not stalling before beginning your work.

As I mentioned earlier, we here in the United States work way too much. We put in more work hours than anyone in the industrialized world -- even the so-called workaholic Japanese! We also take the least vacation of anyone else in the industrialized world. The sad part is that we are no more productive than people in these other countries. In fact, many experts have found that we accomplish less during a work day than people in other developed societies.

So try not to fool yourself that you need to work around the clock. Sometimes you need to be creative to find solutions to your complicated lifestyle.

As with anything else, becoming aware of your reasons for continuing to work too hard are the first steps to dismantling the habit. Make note of the above examples and add a few of your own as necessary. There are likely as many reasons for dramatizing the number of hours you need to work to meet your goals as there are people on the planet.

EXERCISE:

Find something to anchor your day. Part of the reason we lose focus and flounder is because we lack structure. I personally notice that having a few practical busy tasks that I need to do like driving my kid to school or making dinner every night, keep me more focused on ALL the things I need to do on any given day. When I just roll out of bed and head for the computer, I'm much more likely to get lost in email and web surfing before getting to any actual work.

Be creative. Host an Internet radio show for 30 minutes even just once a week, make an appointment to meet a potential offline client or take an exercise class. Whatever you choose, it must be something that needs to be accomplished at a specific time. Having that commitment will help you to get the juices flowing to accomplish more in your day.

MORAL:

When you sit down to work, make sure you actually work. It is easy to get sidetracked by small busy tasks. Whenever possible, try to minimize those tasks by delegating them to someone who is capable of seeing them through with little or no error.

15 - The Naysayer

"When in doubt, don't." - Benjamin Franklin

When you start working on a new method or project, do you have this little nagging voice telling you that you cannot progress until you have the last piece of the puzzle? If so, then you are not alone. This is just one more way that your ego attempts to keep us in our current state of stagnation and complaining that we cannot get ahead without some external piece of information.

If this sounds like you, then you need to stop playing the blame game and reach down into your own creativity to find the missing links. Remember, you do not want to copy what others are doing exactly anyway. Can you imagine what would happen if a thousand people tried to launch the identical product or service simultaneously?

Think of it this way, your doctor does not know everything about medicine in order to open a practice. Lawyers, mechanics, plumbers, bankers and people in just about any profession cannot possibly know everything about their respective line of work, but that certainly does not stop them from making money at it.

Chances are that part of your pursuit for intellectual perfection stems from a fear of being ridiculed. I know this is a challenge for me. Then one day I realized that people were ridiculing me when I barely had two nickels to rub together, so why should it be any more hurtful to know that people are talking bad about me behind my back when I do have money? The only difference is that I would be rich and ridiculed instead of broke. I can live with that. You probably can too.

The best course of action to take in this case is to get started, even if you need to start small and feel your way around your moneymaking process at the beginning. Then as your business gets off the ground, you can further your learning on the side through books, conferences and mentors.

Just like I tell my assistants, "You cannot be successful without being resourceful." Do not let your internal objections get the best of you. The more excuses you give yourself to not start on your moneymaking mission right now, the more likely you will be to give up on your lifelong dreams.

EXERCISE:

This is a role-playing exercise I learned from a neurolinguistic programming specialist. It can work wonders for your productivity by forcing you to look at yourself in an objective way. When this happens, your ego must take a backseat to your conscious mind.

Before I proceed to explain the technique though, I would caution you that if you have any demons in your closet that you should ONLY do this in the presence of a trained therapist as it may have the potential of bringing some ugly sentiments to the forefront of your mind. Do not take this warning lightly. This is powerful stuff.

This is how it works:

Choose a location in the room where you are to sit or stand in. Look at any other location in the room and discuss whatever comes to mind regarding your productivity. Talk as if you are in the location you are facing, not where you are actually standing. For example, you might say, "What are you waiting for? Why can't you make a go of your invention? If you would just turn off the TV, you would be a success by now! You've been at it for 3 years now. Enough is enough…"

When you have finished having your say with your "other" self, move to the location you were speaking to and answer the questions or assertions made while facing the part of the room you were standing in previously. So in this case, your response might be something like "I do not know. I start working every day thinking I'm going to get things done, but I cannot. I feel lost. I need more information. I'm so busy that I get confused….."

You can keep going back and forth between the two locations talking to yourself back and forth, uncovering what it is that is deepest within you. This will bring tremendous clarity to your goals, as well as a sharp increase in your productivity.

You could even record the session and play it back later so that you can fully be in the moment while you are speaking. Later when you listen, you will be able to objectively pinpoint the real reasons why you make certain decisions and how to change things around for the better.

When I first did this exercise, I was stunned later to realize that I completely took on a different persona in each location I chose. In one place I was authoritative and secure with straight posture. In the other location I was crying my eyes out and slouched over feeling pathetic and somewhat ashamed of my behavior (lack of productivity, that is).

Later that afternoon, I took a much needed nap and when I woke up, the crying me had vanished and I became super productive. I even made a huge dinner in 45 minutes that would normally take at least 2 hours to make!

MORAL:

Your ego likes to complain and will do anything to maintain the status quo. Become aware of these internal objections and make the decision to be creative and resourceful. Awareness and unconscious behavior cannot coexist. As you become aware, you will be able to make positive decisions to move forward in any challenge you take on.

16 - A Good Use of Ego

"Always imitate the behavior of the winners when you lose."
- George Meredith, writer

Although I spent this entire book explaining how the ego gets the most of you and strives to keep you in your current situation, you can also use the ego to your advantage. This is sort of like getting even.

Think of all those people who doubt you or even laugh at you. Use their mocking attitudes and rolling eyes as fuel to keep you focused on your work. Imagine their faces when you tell them that you are finally able to quit your day job and travel the world or otherwise do whatever the heck you want with your time while they continue to slave away at their nine to five job. Get even with them by having the last laugh.

I am sure that many people reading this will think this is a childish and pathetic stance to take. Of course it is! This is after all the ego we are talking about. This is the very thing that the ego does best.

It is very difficult to become entirely free of the ego. So if you are going to be encumbered by this entity, it would behoove you to use it to your benefit until you let go of it.

Another way to do this is to create a new story of who you are. It seems today that everyone is in competition to have a sad story about their life.

A few years ago, I befriended a woman who wallowed in the thought of having been neglected as a child. She would go on for hours about how her mother would not send her and her brother to school and then would lie about it to their dad, how she raised her brother, taught him to read (even though nobody supposedly taught her to read), how she gave him his first job etc. She considered herself the only responsible one in her family.

At face value, she seemed to have created a new story of who she was, however, her determination to hold on to this sad childhood story clearly impacted her current life. She and her husband were unemployed for over two years, they had an autistic child and her marriage seemed more like a practical arrangement than a love relationship.

The scariest part is that she would compare her childhood story to that of others by saying things like "That's nothing compared to my childhood." All I could think was, "Why the competition?" Has pain and suffering become the new mode of bragging? Sadly, for many it has.

Just as my friend, Kris, whom I mentioned earlier in the book blamed her less-than-ideal childhood and everyone around her for her poor relationship with her parents and her failed marriage, many people create a story about themselves that focuses on limitations set by some past injustice. The difference is that Kris acknowledged her role in her then current state of misery and re-wrote her story by blessing and releasing past pain.

Instead of repeating the mantra that she had such a painful childhood, she developed a story of being a strong and powerful woman. What served her in the past no longer worked for the person that she wanted to be. We could all benefit from this type of shift.

If the ego loves drama so much, then give it good drama to feed off of. What would you prefer? The drama of not being able to pay your bills, feed your family the quality of food you prefer, or buy a house? Or would you prefer the drama of trying to decide whether to go to Asia or Europe for your next vacation? Or whether or not you should by the red or blue Bugatti?

Without the ego many people would not achieve their goals and you should be no different. Just make sure that your ego is truly serving the successful you, not the one who will always be drawn back into some past story of hurt and dismay.

17 - Lesson from Babes: Finding a Place for Failure

"Mistakes are almost always of a sacred nature. Never try to correct them. On the contrary: rationalize them, understand them thoroughly. After that, it will be possible for you to sublimate them."
- Salvador Dali

I know the subtitle of this book is "Success Secrets that Go Beyond Positive Thinking & The Law of Attraction", but failure happens to most, if not all, of us at some point on our road to success. The problem is when we refuse to use failure as fuel to succeed.

As an infant, nobody learns to crawl, walk and talk on day one. Babies fall and pronounce words badly sometimes for years before they get the hang of it. But do they just throw in the towel and say "Walking didn't work for me today, so I'm just gonna give up and let people carry me for the rest of my life."? No. They try different strategies until they get it right or at least as close to "right" as possible so they can be understood or get from point A to point B quickly.

Remember how the ego likes to be right at all costs? Well, that is precisely what is happening here.

The baby does not accept that it cannot achieve what people around him have, so the ego gives him the drive to attain at least as much as the others he is observing. This is a wonderful example to follow.

Like the baby, you can decide now that making an unlimited income is possible because others have done it or you can allow your ego to wallow in self-pity by deciding that it is too hard or not worth it to become financially secure. The choice is yours.

The first path might take some self-discipline, persistence and fine-tuning of skills, but things will absolutely turn out in your favor as long as you remain solution-oriented on your journey. The other path requires no special skills, but a certain level of satisfaction with maintaining the status quo.

In both cases, the ego is involved. No matter which one you choose, the ego will prove itself right.

On average, most babies walk by 12 months. That's right, from zero to walking in 12 months. They begin talking clearly between 18 months and two years of age. Think of where you would be in 12 or 24 months if you kept focusing on getting just a few tasks mastered. And you are not even starting from zero. You probably have at least 20 years of experience (read: age) to create your empire.

So here's the question:

Would you rather be right and broke? Or wrong and rich?

18 - The Challenge

"A man is not old until regrets take the place of dreams."
- John Barrymore, actor

By now, I hope you can recognize just how powerful you are and how simple it can be to achieve success by changing the way you think. There is definitely more of a learning curve for some people than for others, but that is no reason to throw in the towel.

Two more quick stories before I let you go.

When I was 25, I lost a very dear friend to AIDS. He never was able to visit me in the United States, which was his lifelong dream.

In 2010, another friend suddenly died from liver cancer that had only been diagnosed two months prior. He had just turned 44. He never married or had children as he had always told me he wanted to.

Life is short even when it is not cut short by disease or an accident. Make sure you live out your dreams while you can. Recognize the power within you to make success happen to you. Remember that you deserve the best, but in most cases will need to steer the ship in the right direction to get what's coming to you.

The ball is in your court. Will you convince yourself that the methods in this book do not work and continue to live in your current reality? Will you think this book makes some good points, but go back to doing things the old ineffective way using the mindset that has proven not to serve you? Or will you reset your mindset and dare to dream dreams only limited by your imagination?

Final Notes and Resources

To find out more about Internet marketing and my journey to success, go to http://imarketingspy.com. There you can get a free copy of my report "Money at Your Fingertips" and learn about how to start making money online in as little as five minutes. You can also join my Facebook fan page at http://www.facebook.com/selfemploymentideas to get advice on how to begin a new career online.

If you do not yet have any money-generating ideas that will liberate you from your day job and Internet marketing is not of interest to you, then I suggest you pick up a copy of The Four-Hour Work Week by Tim Ferriss. This book is overflowing with ideas on unique money-making ideas and resources. So if your aim is to make more money than you do in your current job, The Four-Hour Work Week will help you generate a ton of business ideas to explore.

For a more in-depth analysis of the ego, Eckhart Tolle's A New Earth is a must. As you read this book, be prepared for many "a-ha" moments as the author reveals the forgotten meanings of popular spiritual and philosophical texts.

If you are interested in improving your relationship with money, Morgana Rae has my highest recommendation. There are a lot of charlatans in this field, but what Morgana teaches not only makes sense, *it works!* You can check out her Money Magnet Breakthrough Pack at http://imarketingspy.com/morgana.

And lastly, if you are looking for a more esoteric read, then check out Ask and It Is Given by Esther and Jerry Hicks. The main subject matter of the text will require many people to suspend their belief systems, however, the money attracting exercises are excellent.

ABOUT THE AUTHOR

Adrienne Hew is a holistic Certified Nutritionist and linguist turned Internet marketer. Born to Jamaican immigrants, she has always been taught to recognize the United States as the land where anyone can become anything he or she desires. Since studying the concepts behind the "law of attraction" in 2006, her family has experienced rapid and dramatic increases in income and good fortune. She currently resides in New Jersey with her husband and two children and travels every chance she gets.

Printed in Great Britain
by Amazon